David Boventer

Vocation

Bibliographical information on the National German Library System:
The German National library lists this publication in the German National Bibliography, detailed bibliographical data may be researched on the internet at http://dnb.dnb.de

Bibliografische Information der Deutschen Nationalbibliothek:
Die Deutsche Nationalbibliothek verzeichnet diese Publikation in der Deutschen Nationalbibliografie; detaillierte bibliografische Daten sind im Internet über http://dnb.dnb.de abrufbar.

© 2016 David Boventer Illustrations: By my kids, Otto Scholtes and Nasa. NASA, ESA, J. Dalcanton, B. F. Williams (University of Washington, USA), L. C. Johnson (University of Washington, USA), the PHAT team, and R. Gendler. ESA/Hubble & NASA, Acknowledgement: Serge Meunier

Herstellung und Verlag: BoD – Books on Demand, Norderstedt

ISBN: 9783739225043

CONTENTS

Melting our days

Basic needs

Vocation

Pace

Pillar of worlds

David Martin Boventer was born in November 1963 in the beautiful city of Freiburg in Southern Germany in the midst of the Black Forest. His home was a binational cradle of German-American culture and global literacy. Natural Sciences, Politics and Philosophy created an intense intellectual power current and strait of discussion. The joy of dissent and the plight for harmony as demanded by the intercultural dialogue formed an athmosphere where art was inspiration and longing for knowledge.

„**This book is a seperate poetical entity, which unfolded itself while resisting a mere transliteration. Respecting the autonomy of every language, however universal in its lineage and heritage, meant giving in to its inner tension and beauty**".

David Boventer has mastered in German philology and addtional certificates in Business administration, Political Science and as a Software and IT-Specialist. He is currently working as an independent entrepreneur.

Illustrations by his children, by Otto Scholtes and by the observant mechanical servants of Nasa.

Melting our days

Keys spark mightily
casting shadows green
the beginning knows its sister
letters change despicably
while the pulse has a roaring echo

Voices stretch the treetops
twisted branches in suspension
and in the midst of rain
Earth geometrically clothes itself
like a rush of sand
until the shell demands entry
the waves rock the fish into
their sleep

Keys fervently form
as the light wispers
names and vacuum while
insight resists reflections
emanating from multitude
from the prism of hope
until our days melt away
the frozen night

Basic needs (I)

Quiet, oh
humming fear
crescent void
creeps within
knocking out reason
and bridal thoughts
the plight has wings
seeding the merry
before
dust widows us
we request
a line of horizontal light
to be thwarted
across
a celestial tempest
of life

Basic needs (II)

Ubiquitous is our mask
so tenderly wished afar
a sigh and a thought
but in granit we engrain
the call for freedom

Without echo
no angry voice walks beyond
entangled in joy
life paints over
the canvas of creation
thirst and a bolt
split our dark desires
until the morning
grows old

Vocation (I)

Be without fright
the calling has a door
and the name its place
in the palm of comfort

On the threshold
of our nightly mares
stands the guardian
of sleep
joining the pulse
passed away with the
blade of perfection
yet to be seen

Nothing may remain
nor may breath the same air
hence the human countenance
must fall into the maelstrom
of memory and creation

Vocation (II)

Your knowledge will complete
and modesty will flee
in veneration of the Almighty
in rage of iteration
of countless crimes
and hope can mould anew
to the blushing novelty of age

Be without fright
when your world bursts
while stars and restless suns
counsel you
and the father of time
calls you son of G-D.

Pace

Escaping the material cave
images and voices conquer
the riverbed of my senses
and above the coloring ocean
a grey dome spurs dreams
of space and expansion

In the reign of options
insight steers
a tumultuous course
and essence opens its suspense
between time and clock

The pillar of worlds

Escaping the chaff of dust
while wind sorts the heartful minds
HIS pounding beats
the ore of our senses

Neither waft of weather
nor hugging of ground
does comfort the hollow view
from pillar to pillar we crawl
alongside the wall of worlds

Earth embraces the fallen words
on barren land
roots do not breed
and the curse of repetition
scourges our confidence

The pillar of worlds (II)

Where the desert kisses its sun
dawn gives its bread
with trembling hands
we cast the anchor
until the skies fear our might

Swift waft of weather
a gentle stroke of ground
and the quill of thought awakens
thy ancient novelty with weary eyes
hardly squinting in torturing light

The storm laughs at us
and above the clouds
certainty claims its name
stone bears fire
the flame which leads our way